Sh*t My Students Say

a journal for teachers

To all the teachers who have to deal with some crazy sh*t.
Thank you.

Copyright © 2018 by BootsTees
www.BootsTees.com
All rights reserved.
ISBN: 9781726621007

Date: _____

So this shit happened...

Date: _____

So this shit happened...

Date: _____

So this shit happened...

Date:

Date: _____

So this shit happened...

Date: _____

So this shit happened...

So this shit happened... Date: _____

Date:

Date:

Date:

Date: _____

So this shit happened...

Date: _____

So this shit happened...

Date: _____

So this shit happened...

Date: _____

So this shit happened...

Date: _____

So this shit happened...

Date: _____

So this shit happened...

Date: _____

So this shit happened...

Date: _____

So this shit happened...

Date: _____

So this shit happened...

Date:

Date:

Date: _____

So this shit happened...

Date: _____

So this shit happened...

Date: _____

So this shit happened...

Date: _____

So this shit happened...

Date: _____

So this shit happened...

Date: _____

So this shit happened...

Date: _____

So this shit happened...

Date: _____

So this shit happened...

Date: _____

So this shit happened...

So this shit happened...   Date: _____

Date:

Date:

Date: _____

So this shit happened...

Date: _____

So this shit happened...

Date: _____

So this shit happened...

So this shit happened...   Date: _____

Date: _____

So this shit happened...

Date: _____

So this shit happened...

Date: _____

So this shit happened...

Date: _____

So this shit happened...

Date: _____

So this shit happened...

Date: _____

So this shit happened...

Date: _____

So this shit happened...

Date: _____

So this shit happened...

Date: _____

So this shit happened...

Date: _____

So this shit happened...

Date: _____

So this shit happened...

Date:

Date: _____

So this shit happened...

Date: _____

So this shit happened...

Date: _____

So this shit happened...

Date: _____

So this shit happened...

Date: _____

So this shit happened...

Date: _____

So this shit happened...

Date: _____

So this shit happened...

Date: _____

So this shit happened...

Date:

Date:

Date: _____

So this shit happened...

And that's the end of that shit.

Made in the USA
Middletown, DE
24 April 2022

64693572R00073